Animals of North America
MOOSE

by Christy Mihaly

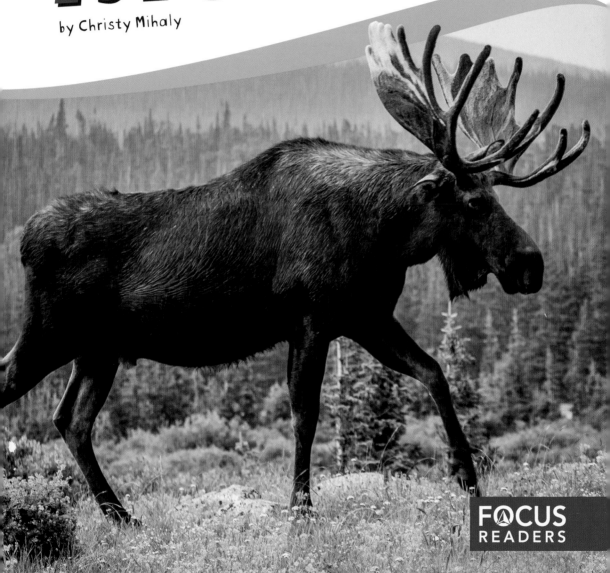

FOCUS READERS

www.northstareditions.com

Produced for North Star Editions by Red Line Editorial.

Photographs ©: MEGiordano_Photography/iStockphoto, cover, 1; Oliver S/Shutterstock Images, 4–5; Patrik Kiefer/iStockphoto, 6; Paul Tessier/iStockphoto, 9; goldistocks/iStockphoto, 10–11; Drakuliren/Shutterstock Images, 13, 29; Diane Picard/Shutterstock Images, 14; visceralimage/Shutterstock Images, 16–17; Carol Gering/iStockphoto, 20–21; Malgorzata Litkowska/Shutterstock Images, 22; TheGreenMan/Shutterstock Images, 24–25, 27 (left); kosmos111/Shutterstock Images, 27 (top); Rocky Grimes/Shutterstock Images, 27 (right); BGSmith/Shutterstock Images, 27 (bottom)

ISBN
978-1-63517-035-1 (hardcover)
978-1-63517-091-7 (paperback)
978-1-63517-194-5 (ebook pdf)
978-1-63517-144-0 (hosted ebook)

Library of Congress Control Number: 2016951007

Printed in the United States of America
Mankato, MN
November, 2016

About the Author

Christy Mihaly has been lucky enough to observe moose in the wilds of Maine, New Hampshire, Wyoming, Alaska, and near her home in Vermont. She has a degree in environmental studies and writes about nature, science, and other topics for readers of all ages.

TABLE OF CONTENTS

CHAPTER 1

MEET THE MOOSE

A huge moose climbs out of a lake, dripping with water. The animal shakes off. Water flies from its long, large nose. Its big ears wiggle.

 An adult moose stands approximately 6 to 7 feet (1.8 to 2.1 m) tall.

▷ **The moose is the largest animal in the deer family.**

The moose has long, skinny legs and antlers as big as a bicycle. Moose measure approximately 10 feet (3.0 m) long. That is longer than most couches.

Adult male moose are called bulls. A large bull can weigh more than 1,300 pounds (590 kg). Adult females are called cows. A cow weighs approximately 600 to 800 pounds (270 to 360 kg). A new **calf** weighs approximately 30 pounds (14 kg).

FUN FACT

Moose move their ears separately. They turn them every way to check for sounds coming from all directions.

GROWING AND SHEDDING ANTLERS

Each spring, little knobs appear on a bull moose's head. These tiny bumps grow up to 1 inch (2.5 cm) every day. Antlers are made of bone and are covered in a fuzzy skin. They grow in symmetric pairs, meaning both sides of the antlers look the same. A pair of antlers can weigh more than 40 pounds (18 kg).

Once the antlers are formed, bull moose rub their antlers against trees to scrape the fuzz off. The moose's strong antlers are important in fall. During **mating season**, bulls use their antlers to fight each other

Moose antlers can spread wider than 6 feet (1.8 m) across.

for females. Moose shed their antlers in winter. Squirrels, mice, and other animals eat them. New antlers will come in the next year.

CHAPTER 2

WHAT'S USEFUL TO A MOOSE?

Moose may look a bit funny, but their bodies are well adapted for northern areas of North America. They are built to live through cold, snowy winters. They also are well suited for water and mud.

 A moose's thick fur keeps it warm during winter.

Moose have big hooves. Moose hooves can measure up to 5.5 inches (14 cm) across and 7 inches (18 cm) long. Large hooves are useful for walking on snow. They help moose paddle through the water, too. Moose have two **dewclaws** on the back of each foot.

PARTS OF A MOOSE

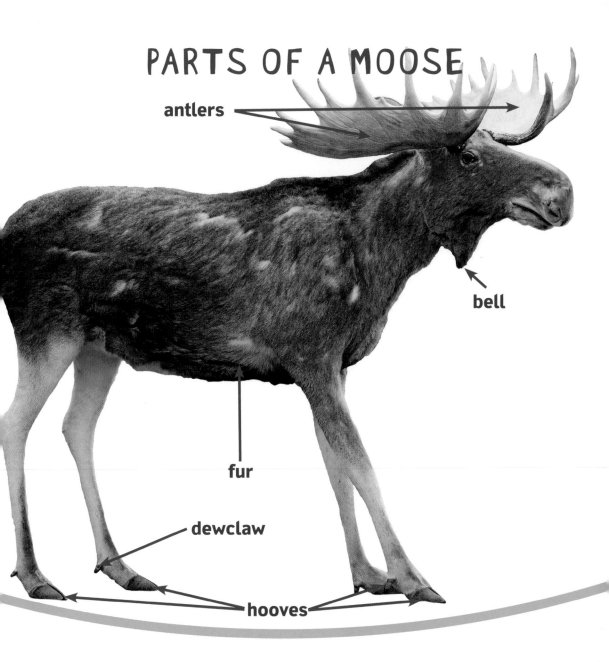

antlers

bell

fur

dewclaw

hooves

These stick out and keep the moose from sinking into soft mud.

A moose trudges through deep snow.

Moose legs are long. They help the moose walk easily over logs in the forest and through deep snow in winter.

A flap of fur-covered skin hangs under the moose's chin. It is called a bell.

A moose's fur is thick and contains hollow hairs. The air in the hairs keeps the moose warm in winter. In summer, the fur helps the moose float while swimming.

CHAPTER 3

MOOSE ON THE LOOSE

Moose are at home in cold places, making North America a perfect place for them to live. Many moose live in Canada and Alaska. The moose's **range** also reaches across the northern United States.

Some moose live in the Rocky Mountains.

Moose live in forests and other areas of wilderness, where there are plenty of plants to eat. In summer, moose seek out rivers, lakes, and **wetlands**. Sometimes they climb into the mountains to escape insects and **predators**.

FUN FACT

A moose can roll its eyes up, down, and all around, even in two different directions at once.

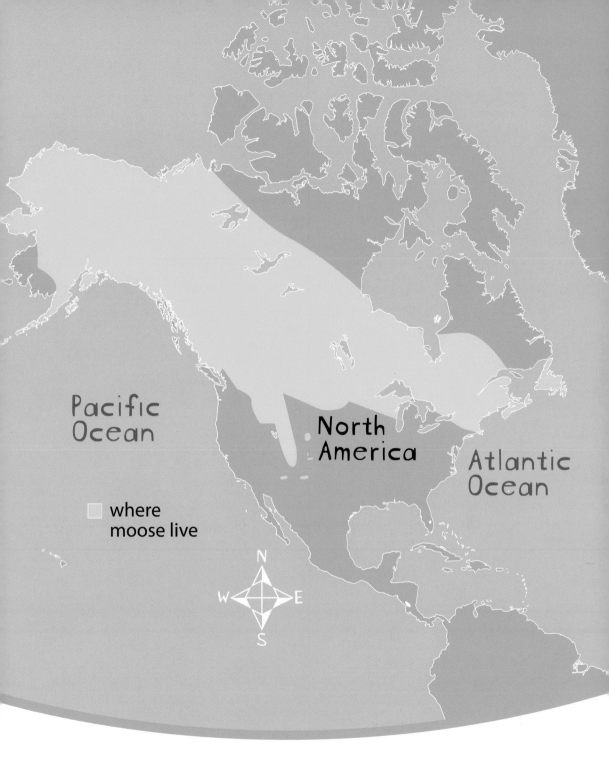

Pacific
Ocean

North
America

Atlantic
Ocean

☐ where
moose live

N
W E
S

 Moose live mostly in Alaska and Canada.

CHAPTER 4

WHAT DO MOOSE DO?

Moose are herbivores. That means they eat plants. Moose eat many kinds of leaves, stems, and buds. During summer, they eat plants that grow in the water.

A moose chomps on leaves.

> Moose often walk into water to eat water lilies and other plants.

In winter, they strip bark from trees and eat it.

Moose do not form large herds. A group may gather where there is plenty of food. And a calf stays with its mother. But moose usually live alone.

Moose are strong swimmers. They often walk into water to cool off or get away from biting insects. Calves learn to swim when they are just a few days old.

Wolves, grizzly bears, and black bears hunt moose. But adult moose are big, and they fight with their feet. Kicking with sharp hooves, a moose can send a predator running.

CHAPTER 5

MOOSE REPRODUCE

Each spring, moose cows give birth to one or two calves. The cows give their calves milk. They also teach them to find food. The moose eat all summer long.

 A cow nuzzles her calf.

In fall, bulls fight, crashing their antlers against each other. Cows watch and choose mates.

In winter, food is hard to find. The moose lie down in loose, fluffy snow to keep warm. When spring returns, calves leave their mothers. Moose **reproduce** each spring.

MOOSE LIFE CYCLE

Calves are born in spring. They spend the summer eating and learning from their mothers.

One-year-old calves are ready to leave their mothers.

Bulls fight each other and mate with cows in fall.

Moose rest in winter.

FOCUS ON
MOOSE

Write your answers on a separate piece of paper.

1. Write a letter to a friend describing what you learned about moose.

2. Would you be surprised to see a moose where you live? Why or why not?

3. Approximately how big are a bull moose's antlers?
   - A. the size of a skateboard
   - B. the size of a bicycle
   - C. the size of a car

4. What might happen if a calf didn't stay with its mother for the first year?
   - A. The calf might not grow antlers.
   - B. The calf might not shed its antlers in winter.
   - C. The calf might not learn how to find food.

5. What does **hollow** mean in this book?

    A. full and thick

    B. long

    C. empty inside

A moose's fur is thick and contains **hollow** hairs. The air in the hairs keeps the moose warm in winter.

6. What does **adapted** mean in this book?

    A. too old to live in a particular place

    B. well prepared to live in a particular place

    C. too tall to live in a particular place

Moose may look a bit funny, but their bodies are well **adapted** for northern areas of North America. They are built to live through cold, snowy winters.

Answer key on page 32.

29

GLOSSARY

calf
A baby or young moose.

dewclaws
Small extra hooves on the back of a moose's foot.

mating season
The time of year when animals find mates and pair up.

predators
Animals that kill and eat other animals.

range
The area where a certain kind of animal naturally lives.

reproduce
To give birth to babies.

wetlands
Areas of land that have a lot of moisture, such as marshes or swamps.

TO LEARN MORE

BOOKS

Borgert-Spaniol, Megan. *Moose*. Minneapolis: Bellwether Media, 2015.

Meister, Cari. *Do You Really Want to Meet a Moose?* Mankato, MN: Amicus Ink, 2016.

Owen, Ruth. *Moose*. New York: Windmill Books, 2014.

NOTE TO EDUCATORS

Visit **www.focusreaders.com** to find lesson plans, activities, links, and other resources related to this title.

INDEX

A
antlers, 6, 8–9, 26

B
bell, 15
bulls, 7, 8, 26, 27

C
calves, 7, 22, 23, 25–27
cows, 7, 25–27

D
dewclaws, 12

E
ears, 5, 7

F
food, 22, 25, 26
fur, 15

L
legs, 6, 14

P
predators, 18, 23

R
range, 17

S
snow, 11, 12, 14, 26
swim, 15, 23

Answer Key: 1. Answers will vary; **2.** Answers will vary; **3.** B; **4.** C; **5.** C; **6.** B